HOW WE BECAME WINE SNOBS

L Michael Lavender
Leslie Lavender

Copyright © 2020 L Michael Lavender

All rights reserved

The characters and events portrayed in this book are fictitious. Any similarity to real persons, living or dead, is coincidental and not intended by the author.

No part of this book may be reproduced, or stored in a retrieval system, or transmitted in any form or by any means, electronic, mechanical, photocopying, recording, or otherwise, without express written permission of the publisher.

ISBN-13: 9798682508846

Cover design by: Art Painter
Library of Congress Control Number: 2018675309
Printed in the United States of America

CONTENTS

Title Page	1
Copyright	2
How We became wine snobs	5
Preface	7
Our Journey Begins	12
The Only Way to Cross	15
The First of Many Firsts	21
The French Connection	28
Things We Have Learned	35
Red Wine – A Basic Food Group	40
Final Words	44
Glossary of Wine Terms	46
Thumbnail Sketch of Wines	49
Afterword	57
Acknowledgement	59
About The Author	61

HOW WE BECAME
WINE SNOBS

PREFACE

What exactly is a wine snob? The overall consensus is "a person who believes they know everything there is to know about wine." A typical stereotype would be an extremely passionate, overly enthusiastic, pretentious, self-appointed individual who truly believes they have a vast knowledge about wine and wine making. I rather enjoy being a devil's advocate, so I ask, "Why someone would call an individual a *wine snob* simply because they know more about wine than you?"

I never aspired to be a *wine snob*, but like it or not, my closest friends and relatives are convinced that I am. My wife, Leslie, agrees, and admits, that she has become one too.

My initial desire was only to be able to look at a wine list and confidently order an appropriate dinner wine to compliment the meal. It was never my intention to draw attention to myself or appear as a *know it all.* My wife and I have been educators throughout our long medical careers, and we love to impart knowledge on students regarding any area of life that we have learned to enjoy and appreciate. Being *baby boomers*, we have parents, also teachers, who instilled in us ideals and standards for protocol, etiquette, and behavior that has governed our lives.

Wine was not popular in our 1950s and 60s middle-class, suburban lives. We both knew Italian families where wine played an essential part of family life, particularly with meals. The impression of wine for us during that time was that it's a part of celebrations and usually consumed in elegant restaurants. I never even tasted wine until I was in college and what I sampled was not particularly appealing. I actually preferred iced-tea with meals.

I was a graduate medical student when I drank my first enjoyable glass of wine while visiting in Asheville, North Carolina. Attending a regional research competition with several of my professors, I presented a scientific paper and won first prize. To celebrate, we went to dinner in an upscale restaurant and my primary research advisor recommended that we have a good bottle of wine. He asked me if I preferred red or white. Knowing very little about wine but aware that whites were served chilled, I told him I preferred a white. He looked at the wine list and recommended a favorite of his – Pouilly-Fuissé. He remarked that when he was in college it was very reasonably priced but as its popularity had increased, so had the cost. I can't recall the price on the wine list but I'm fairly sure in the seventies, it was around $10 or $12 a bottle. To my amazement, I thought the wine was extraordinary. I later learned that I had tasted and enjoyed my first bottle of Chardonnay from a sub-region of Burgundy in central France.

I was born in Cincinnati, Ohio, and my wife and I grew up in Northern Kentucky. It was not until late in our adult lives that we learned that the first commercial winery in the United States was founded in Cincinnati in the early 1800s. This Midwestern city had a large German-immigrant population and it was these immigrants that were instrumental in developing this first wine industry in the United States.

Likewise, wineries started in Kentucky as early as 1798. Jean Jacques Dufour, an immigrant from Switzerland, planted his first vineyard on the banks of the Kentucky River in central Kentucky and appropriately named it *First Vineyard*. Wine, from Dufour's first press was sent to President Thomas Jefferson in 1805. Unfortunately, frost destroyed most of his vineyard in 1809 and he moved his enterprise to Indiana.

It is interesting to note that Thomas Jefferson was respected as the most knowledgeable wine connoisseur of his day. As foreign minister to France in 1785, he took time off and traveled incognito by horseback for three months visiting Bordeaux, Burgundy, and other wine regions in France and Italy. He appreciated the traditions and unique wines of each region. As a result, he was also largely responsible for introducing wine to the United

States. In addition to his own presidency, he served as a wine advisor to three other presidents.

Sadly, in 1920, Prohibition began and destroyed the winemaking industry including close to 2,500 vineyards across the U.S. Prohibition was repealed in 1933; however, less than 100 vineyards remained. A majority of the expert winemakers were lost to death or old age and the previous vineyards were either neglected or replanted with other crops.

Even though my wife and I were reared in this area, its rich history was unfortunately forgotten and unknown to us. Table wine, which was commonplace in so many homes before 1930, was gone. Our parents were born during the 1920s. They grew up without table wine and my wife and I were now another generation removed. The only wine that we remember while growing up was of extremely cheap quality or very sweet – two features that we cared little for.

The comeback for wine in the United States is attributed to Robert Gerald Mondavi (1913-2008) whose marketing strategies achieved worldwide recognition for the wines of Napa Valley in California. Truly an entrepreneur, like so many immigrants of his era, he experimented with new and better ways to make wine. He had a lot of leeway since there were no strict rules to adhere to in California like there were in Europe. Wines in Europe (Old World) were usually named after the region where they were produced. Mondavi encouraged labeling wines by the principal grape in the bottle rather than the region where they were grown. This has now become the standard for New World wines.

Over the past couple of decades, we have seen a proliferation of wineries in the United States. Competition has resulted in more options for the consumer and globalization has brought a wider variety of wines to the states. With more selections available, more reasonable prices, and more restaurants offering good wines, the popularity in wine consumption has noticeably increased. Wine is now an essential part of American culture.

There is an old adage, "*Wine improves with age,*" but more recently a significant number of individuals believe, "*age im-*

proves with wine!" Consequently, in addition to family meals, social events, and celebrations, people now drink red wine for health benefits. Although there are conflicting opinions regarding conclusive claims about red wine consumption, a plethora of scientific research has shown definite benefits, particularly in decreasing cardiovascular disease. Opponents are still not convinced, and the debate will most likely go on indefinitely.

Knowledge of wine is similar to the knowledge of the fine arts, such as music, painting, sculpture, and literature. The more we study and learn, the more we appreciate. So, why are individuals in the U.S. who are knowledgeable about wine considered pretentious?

The reappearance of wine in American culture came in like a storm. No social strata were exempt. In contrast, wine appreciation in Europe has a long tradition going back millennia. To various European countries, their homelands were the birthplace of wine. Their long history, tradition, and decorum established rules. The vast majority of twenty-first century Americans do not want to be told how to enjoy their new liquid refreshment or comply with rules they were never privy to.

My wife and I try not to look like wine snobs in public. I don't believe that we over-swirl our glasses at restaurants, although we do at home. Swirling definitely aerates the wine and opens up the flavors over time. Likewise, we don't loudly sniff our wine in restaurants, but we certainly appreciate the aroma of the wine at home. Inhaling deeply and taking in the most wonderful fragrances is only second best to tasting. Do we chew the wine that we sip with obvious facial movements publicly? Positively not, but at home we love to experience the wonderful flavors that occur when you hold the newly opened wine in your mouth and gently nibble. We describe to each other the flavors that we experience beginning with the first taste as well as throughout the meal. Often our tastes are similar, but sometimes they differ. Each individual has a unique palate for which to appreciate what the wine has to offer.

Admittedly, I do have certain pet peeves. I am annoyed

when individuals openly announce *I only drink white wine* or *I only drink red.* Not only do I insist on the proper stemware, but also I cringe if the wine is served in a glass tumbler or generic wine glass at a nice Italian restaurant. Does temperature of the wine matter? You bet it does. Even if the wine is inexpensive, I don't want my white wine so cold that it frosts the glass; or my red wine at room temperature or even warmer (I'll share with you the appropriate temperatures to serve and drink later). If that's a *wine snob,* then I guess I am one!

I am more relaxed and forgiving in the United States. However, when I am in Europe, I do not want to offend and, as a welcomed guest, I want to be courteous and share in their culture and traditions. Wine etiquette abroad is imperative for American travelers. Leslie and I have been extremely embarrassed on too many occasions in Europe with illiterate American behavior in European wineries and restaurants. Hopefully, we can share appropriate wine protocol and politeness in the coming chapters.

Wine is the most amazing beverage. It has been made in almost every country of the world throughout mankind's existence. My wife and I are certainly not experts on wine, but what we have learned over the past decade, we would like to share with you in these short vignettes.

OUR JOURNEY BEGINS

It was a blind date and neither of us was particularly enthusiastic about the evening to come. Both of us were thinking about other things that they could be doing. In an effort to be a good host, I asked her if she would like to share a bottle of Pinot Noir. She replied reluctantly, "I only drink white – red gives me a headache." And so the journey began.

Twelve years later, as an unlikely but inseparable duo, we have traveled the world. We have tasted the product of many, many grapes. We have learned about wine production beginning in the vineyards through the harvest and bottling of the final product. We have learned how to buy wine, how to store wine, how to serve wine, and how to pair it with food to ensure the maximum enjoyment of this living entity.

If we were reluctant to go on the blind date, we were even more reluctant to part, when, three-and-a-half hours later we suddenly realized we were the only customers left in the dining room. Our servers were polite but anxious for us to leave. Since that time, we have rarely been apart and we were married nine months later.

Early in our relationship, we went to another nice restaurant and, feeling more comfortable with each other, I encouraged Leslie to try a nice Pinot Noir. Because of previous headaches, Leslie was hesitant but wanted to see for herself why I liked this wine so much. The server recommended a medium-priced wine from Sonoma Valley in California. To her surprise, she enjoyed it and couldn't believe how well it complimented the food. Anticipating a headache, she couldn't believe it when she woke up the next morning headache free.

Many people who suffer from headaches after drinking wine are convinced that the discomfort is due to the sulfites in the wine. It is true that sulfites are added to both red and white wines. They prevent spoilage and actually make some reds redder and prevent white wines from turning brown. What most people are unaware of is that white wines generally have more sulfites added than reds. In addition, virtually all wines have sulfites. Sulfites are a natural by-product of the fermentation process. To date, there is no medical evidence that sulfites, either naturally or added to the wines cause headaches. Leslie has now been drinking reds for the past decade and remains headache free. We believe that drinking better wine (not necessarily expensive) has fewer headache triggers. Finally convinced that red wine wouldn't bring on a headache, she was ready to delve deeper into the world of wine.

Leslie and I hadn't been dating long when an anesthesia colleague invited us out to dinner one evening. He knew we were interested in wine and he had just discovered a new Cabernet Sauvignon in a local restaurant. He was anxious for us to try it. He said, "It's really good and very reasonably priced, but as soon as people find out about it, the price is going to go up." Our friend was very knowledgeable about wine and he helped us navigate the menu. The food and the wine complimented each other beautifully. His explanations based on his knowledge of wine and chemistry helped us better understand the relationship between the food and the wine. He explained that many people choose food and wine by flavors that complement each other; however, there are some people who choose food and wine for the contrast. But, that's for the left-brain thinkers.

The evening made me recall an experience I'd had a few years before. I was on the West coast for a medical conference. The meeting ended and all of my colleagues flew home that evening, but my plane didn't leave until the next day. As I walked from the conference center to my hotel, I passed a restaurant that was advertising a dinner with wine parings. I booked a reservation. Throughout several courses, it was amazing when the food and wine were paired together. They had *synergy*, or a third flavor beyond what either the food or drink offered alone.

Excited by our new knowledge and discoveries, we were eager to try something different. Initially, we followed the old school, simple rules of white wine with fish or fowl and red wine with red meat. As we became more confident in our ability to choose, we became more emboldened in our choices. We began to seek out wine experts such as sommeliers, sellers of wine, and knowledgeable servers in restaurants - basically, anybody who could add to our body of knowledge.

We love to travel, and this gave us the opportunity to seek out local vineyards and taste lots of wine. We found that smaller groups gave us more attention and the ability to ask more questions during visits to vineyards. Once the vintner knew we were interested in their product, they opened up because they are always happy to share their love of wine with people who are truly interested. They also added to our food pairings.

As our knowledge increased, so did our confidence. We began planning dinner parties with both the food and wine menus in mind. For instance, for an open house we may just choose one red and one white. We do the same if we know our dinner guests are wine neophytes. For more intimate dinner parties, we will pair a wine with each course and explain to our guests how we made that choice; this includes red, white, Rosé, and sparkling. The purpose of wine with the meal is to complement or contrast. The more you practice the less intimidating wine becomes. As you learn, you become more confident in your choices.

THE ONLY WAY TO CROSS

(With apologies to John Maxtone-Graham)

    A couple of years into our marriage, we realized that Prince William and Kate Middleton totally copied our wedding. We got married in June of 2009 in a small Episcopal Church. The trumpet and organ music were regal and included "The Prince of Denmark's March" and "Beethoven's Movement IV (Ode to Joy)."

    Following the ceremony, we had a champagne brunch. We spent part of our honeymoon at the Goring Hotel, in London, adjacent to Buckingham Palace and purchased wedding gifts for ourselves at Harrods's. Maybe not exactly like William and Kate, you can see where we went with this. We actually started our honeymoon in Boston on July 4th aboard the Queen Mary 2 (QM2) preparing for what would be the first of several transatlantic crossings. We watched the fireworks from Boston Harbor as the ship set sail for Great Britain.

    At the captain's welcome aboard party, we found out that we were one of three newlywed couples on board and the youngest of the newly weds by at least two decades. For our first dinner aboard ship, we chose fish. I found Pouilly-Fuissé on the wine list and decided to order an old friend. Leslie commented that this was probably the first time that she experienced the incredible synergy between food and wine with a white wine.

    We were on board ship for eight days. Three-quarters of our meals were seafood. They included an abundant variety and many different preparations. Not knowing what wine to pair with these unbelievable entrees, we developed a great rapport with the sommelier and learned not to be intimidated. He recommended a variety of whites, rosés, and light reds with the seafood. We were pleased with every choice.

What do you do to occupy your time for eight days at sea? We had wine tastings, classes, and lectures every day. I would highly recommend beginners in wine appreciation to take advantage of these basic classes. Pay close attention and learn proper wine etiquette. Experiencing wine is not limited to tasting, but also how to hold the glass, observe the legs, appreciate the color, techniques for swirling, breathing in the aroma, as well as how to appreciate the flavor.

The starting point for drinking wine begins with holding the wine glass properly. Picture in your mind a wine glass. There is a thin stem rising from a flat base to support a curved glass bowl. This wine glass design was created for a purpose. The glass was meant to be held by the stem. Cupping the bowl at the bottom with the stem between your fingers or grasping the bowl in your hand while drinking from the glass is inappropriate. You will deliver far too much wine in your mouth and go through a glass very quickly. I agree with the French; wine was meant to be enjoyed with food and drunk slowly.

You ALWAYS hold the glass by the stem. Why? As a rule, wines should not be served above 65 degrees Fahrenheit. The glass rod (stem) prevents your warm hand (98.6 degrees) from quickly warming the wine. As it gradually warms when exposed to room temperature, the wine will aerate, steadily peak, and the flavors will be wonderfully enhanced. This slow warming is desired and brings out the flavor and aromas as you drink slowly from the glass.

A good example of this is an experience I had a number of years ago. I was out to dinner with my good friends Steve and Kay at a small, family-run Italian restaurant. My friend ordered a fabulous bottle of Italian red wine. After the glasses were poured, we all tasted the wine. Steve said to me, "As the evening progresses this wine is going to continue to change and get even better." To my amazement, this is exactly what happened.

Many individuals, as well as many restaurants serve, red wine at room temperature. This is too warm. I store red wine at 55 degrees F. and white wine at 45 degrees F. After removing a bottle from the wine refrigerator, I like to allow about 15-20 minutes at room temperature before opening and serving either the red or the white. These temperatures may vary across different climates and different regions of the country. You will need to experiment and find the optimal temperatures for you.

The next most common mistake with serving wine is how much to pour. Most Americans are cavalier and pour far too much. An easy rule to follow is one-third of the glass for red, one-half of the glass for white, and three-quarters of a glass for sparkling or Champagne. Four to five ounces of red wine is an appropriate pour. You should be able to pour five to six servings from a bottle of red wine.

The size of the glass is the next important item to consider. I, personally, like a large glass, particularly for reds. I also prefer only four ounces in the glass. I enjoy swirling the wine frequently to aerate the wine and to appreciate the developing aromas and flavors. Drinking slowly and taking time to swirl allows you to really enjoy and appreciate the wine. The food is enhanced and the wine lasts longer.

Glasses come in all sizes and shapes. Unique wine glasses were designed to enhance the flavors and aromas of the many different types of wine. There are glasses created specifically for Pinot Noir, Chardonnay, Bordeaux, Sauvignon Blanc, Brandy, Burgundy, Rosé, Syrah, Chablis, Champagne, and Port. Again, I don't care for small glasses, stemless glasses, or tumblers. The smaller the glass, the harder it is for the aromas to escape and swirling is inhibited. Larger glasses permit more oxygen to come in contact with the wine, which in turn helps to aerate and open up the wine.

You don't need a glass for every type of wine. For nice dinner parties, we have glasses for red wine, white wine, and Champagne. For buffets and open houses we have a couple of dozen all purpose wine glasses with stems that we keep stored in a closet for the occasion.

Probably the most intimidating experience for an inexperienced wine connoisseur is the ritual of tasting and accepting a bottle of wine that you ordered with your meal. Very few individuals are truly experts in the field of wine. You don't need to overperform and draw attention to the task at hand. The individual who orders the bottle of wine will receive the bottle by the sommelier or server. They will show you the label to verify that this is what you ordered. Simply nod or acknowledge that it is correct. The server will open the bottle and remove the cork. He will hand it to you or place it in front of you. Discretely pick up the cork and examine it without drawing any undue attention. You do not need to sniff the cork. You want to be sure it is wet, insuring the bottle was stored horizontally. I have had sommeliers open the bottle, inspect the cork, and reject the bottle without pouring if the cork was dry. They politely excused themselves and brought another bottle. This has occurred on a couple of rare occasions when expensive bottles were thought to be unacceptable.

If you approve the bottle after examining the cork, the server will pour a small amount of wine into your glass and wait. This is the most intimidating moment. Usually all eyes at the table are directed to you. Don't be nervous, even if you are new to this. Simply swirl the small portion of wine in the glass. Often the lightening is dark in upscale restaurants, but you can raise the glass to appreciate the color. Experienced wine connoisseurs will tilt the glass to examine the *legs* or, as the French say, the *tears*. The glass is tilted and then immediately returned upright. Long streaks will gently roll down the inside of the glass. Yes, long legs are intriguing, but they only really matter to the experts. The longer the legs, the higher the alcohol content of the wine. Wine Masters can actually tell the alcohol content within 0.2% simply by tasting. Leave this for the experts if you are a novice.

Now, bring the glass up to your nose and take a few deep breaths to appreciate the aroma. Better wines usually have a wonderful fragrance. Take a small sip and hold it on your tongue for a few seconds. Don't be in a hurry. Yes, everyone is watching. If the wine is acceptable, simply tell the waiter. If not, tell him what you perceive to be wrong. He will remove the wine. If it is extremely high priced, he may taste the wine himself. If rejected, he will bring you the wine list again and the ritual will be repeated.

If accepted, he will serve everyone at the table before you. Your glass will be filled last and then you or someone else at the table may make a toast to the occasion or everyone's health.

Believe it not, there is a proper etiquette with toasting, and it varies in different parts of the world. One simple rule to follow is to never clink the rims of the glasses. They are thin and fragile and you can easily break fine crystal. Secondly, in many cultures it is impolite to cross arms or hands. Clink with the persons close by, but do not reach across a table to touch everyone's glass. Simply raise your glass and acknowledge the distant person. Always allow the host to go first unless he declines. If you give a toast, it is always polite to acknowledge your host. If you are the host, do not drink to yourself. Be familiar with the local customs and traditions. For example, in Germany, it is highly impolite to not make direct eye contact to those with whom you are toasting.

If you are new to ordering wine, practice at home before performing in public. I rather enjoy the experience, as I get to taste the wine before my guests at the table. Often it leads to interesting conversation.

As Leslie and I reflect back on our wine experiences from our honeymoon and our first transatlantic crossing, I am reminded of one of our guests who presented lectures on the QM2. John Maxtone-Graham was a delightful maritime historian and inspiring lecturer. His extensive knowledge of the many ships that made the transatlantic crossings prior to WWII was both informative and engaging. We enjoyed his lecture so much that we purchased one of his books, *The Only Way to Cross*. The title is a double entendre that we understand so well that we are preparing for our fourth crossing on QM2. It is worth it to us to arrive relaxed and refreshed without jet lag. As the ship moves, so moves the clock.

THE FIRST OF MANY FIRSTS

In the fall of 2012, we were visiting our son who was spending the year studying abroad. After celebrating Thanksgiving with him in Great Britain, we spent a week traveling in Italy. We hired a guide, Gilberto, for several days prior to boarding the Queen Victoria to cruise the Northern Mediterranean.

Our hotel was on the outskirts of Rome in a lovey neighborhood that had lots of families, shops, and outside cafes. The first morning when Gilberto picked us up, he asked how or why we chose our hotel. We explained that we liked to stay away from the heavily touristed areas and preferred to reside among the locals to get a truer sense of the places we visited.

The first night in Rome, we chose a quaint, outside café for dinner. While the indoor dining area was full, we were told we were welcome to eat outdoors as they had heaters and blankets to keep warm. This outside area also quickly filled to capacity. The waiter helped us navigate the menu and recommended we try the house wine, as it was very popular with the locals. As he brought the wine to the table, we realized that the majority of the diners were drinking the same wine. This was our first experience with Nero d'Avola. To our surprise, we found this same wine at Trader Joe's and it was very reasonably priced. We keep it on hand as one of our own house wines. We serve it for casual dinner parties, when we want to pair Italian wine with Italian food, and to show our guests that inexpensive red wine can be quite good and is readily available.

As we traveled throughout Italy, we ate in many small, out of the way restaurants. We typically ordered the local wines, which often times came to the table in small decanters as opposed to bottles. We found that when we paired the local wines with the local food, both were delicious.

Another surprise for our palates was the discovery of Limoncello in southern Italy. It is often enjoyed after the meal. It is very refreshing and has a slightly cloudy appearance. We were told this was due to the essential oils in the lemon suspended in the alcohol. This liquor has been enjoyed in this region for over one hundred years.

Rome is an inland city. The nearest port on the Mediterranean Sea is in the ancient town of Civitavecchia, about 37 miles from Rome. It was here that we boarded the *Queen Victoria* and said goodbye to Gilberto, who gifted us with a bottle of Limoncello.

We were pleasantly surprised when we found a note in our cabin that gave us a shipboard credit of $400. Not particularly interested in jewelry or garments in the shops, we decided to use the money to buy wine for our dinners. That evening we met Marissa, our sommelier from Eastern Europe. She helped us choose an appropriate wine to compliment our evening meal. We found her to be very knowledgeable and her suggestions were extremely helpful. We shared our interest in trying some of the more expensive wines. Since we had become more interested in wine, we were curious to see if the expensive wines were better.

The answer to that is *probably* and *it depends.* A wine's price does not necessarily reflect its quality. A winery's featured wine price may be exaggerated to make the consumer think they are getting the best wine. Usually the better wines (more expensive) are at the top of the wine list in a nice restaurant. You work your way down in both cost and quality. That doesn't mean that the wines at the bottom of the list are bad, but there is definitely a difference. Someone with an untrained palate is going to be happy with just about anything on that list, in a reasonably good restaurant. You should, however, be careful of the featured wine

– they may be clearing old wines out of their wine cellar to make room for new stock.

Making wine is an expensive undertaking. You invest in the vineyard and winery. Labors for the harvest and processing are costly. A major expenditure is the oak barrels. Only the highest quality oak is used and the yield is usually two barrels per tree. The oak in France is of the highest quality and costs twice that of a barrel in the United States[1]. Finally, you have to allow for aging. There's an old joke that goes, "How do you make a small fortune in the wine industry? You start with a large fortune!"

Now, let me explain why we prefer better quality wines to inexpensive wines. When touring wineries in Europe and the United States, the guides explain the winemaking process. It is very similar throughout the world. The differences are the grapes and blending processes. Less expensive wines are produced in an entirely different way. These wines are mass-produced in enormous stainless steel vats containing hundreds of gallons of crushed grapes. Very often, oak wood chips are added to mimic the flavor obtained by the aging process in the expensive oak barrels. These wine makers are permitted to add from a list of more than 60 approved government additives to alter color, taste, and consistency. The wine made in this manner is then bottled on assembly lines and sent to stores and restaurants with a price around ten dollars a bottle. In one respect, you are essentially buying colored alcohol.

Let me comment about wine prices in restaurants. The mark-up varies, but in all probability, the price on the wine list is likely double the price of what you could purchase in a nice wine shop. So, a $100 bottle could be acquired for only $40 to $50 outside of the restaurant. Many people only want to purchase a glass of wine with their meal. When buying wine by the glass, it is customary for the restaurant to charge the wholesale price of the bottle on the first glass. This gives you an idea of the cost and quality of the wine. Overall, I would say that it is difficult to find a really good wine for under $15 and ever harder for under $10, although there are good finds on rare occasions. You usually cannot go wrong in the $20 bottle range.

Marissa wanted to help us expand our palates. She recommended trying one of Italy's classic wines, Amarone della Valpolicella, commonly known as Amarone. She explained that outside of Italy, it is often little known and underappreciated. The wine is produced in Northern Italy and made from the ripest Corvina grapes. The Corvina grape is known as the queen grape for this wine. Other indigenous grape varieties are mixed with the Corvina grape to produce wonderful added flavors to the Amarone of the region. After the grapes are picked, they are allowed to dry for several weeks. The dried grapes are then pressed. The wines are then matured in oak barrels for a minimum of two years and four years for Reserve, the best quality. Because of the high sugar content in the raisins, the alcohol content is very high, 14 to 16 percent. The wine is exceptionally bold and velvety with wonderful nutty flavors. These wines are paired best with red meat and robust, hearty dishes.

Because of the extensive time and process in producing the wine, be prepared to pay around $60 to $70 a bottle in your local wine store and over $100 a bottle in a nice restaurant. Also be aware of the high alcohol content. This wine is best sipped and enjoyed slowly over dinner.

I need to point out how Marissa introduced us to Amarone. She brought us a menu for the next evening meal. She recommended the lobster and we politely declined. We explained that we only eat fresh lobster, off of the boat, in Maine (that was our full-time residence at the time). We selected prime rib instead. To compliment the red meat, she told us about Amarone which we were anxious to try. To our amazement, she brought the bottle to our table a few minutes later with three wine glasses and poured a small taste in each. It was exceptional. Marissa said, "No, wait until tomorrow night." Then, she poured the entire bottle into a large wine decanter. She swirled the wine vigorously, several times and told us she would bring the wine back tomorrow evening with our meal.

Why was this done? A bold, rich wine like Amarone opens

up even further to release more of the flavors and aromas when decanted and covered the night before. It allows for more oxygen exposure; however, too much oxygen exposure will deaden the flavor of lighter wines. This is why you only decant wines like Amarone or Syrah a day ahead.

Decanters are often used decoratively on an elegant table. You can decant both red and white for your dinner party. In this instance, the decanting can serve two purposes. First, the process allows the removal of unwanted sediments, which can occur naturally in red wines as they age. Secondly, when you decant a lighter wine the aeration often opens up more flavors. These younger wines should be decanted no more than an hour before serving.

There are some fundamental rules that are, for the most part, standard for serving red and white wine. If you are serving both red and white with the meal, serve the white before the red. If you are serving both a younger and an older vintage wine, serve the younger wine first. Drier wines should be served before sweeter wines. The optimal temperature for serving white wine is 45 to 50 degrees Fahrenheit, while red wine is best served at a temperature range of 50 to 60 degrees Fahrenheit. If you are cooling a white wine in the refrigerator (mid to upper 30 degrees), bring it out of the refrigeration 30 to 40 minutes before serving. If your red wine is at room temperature, place it in the refrigerator 30 minutes before serving. By doing this, you can get closer to the desired temperature for the best enjoyment of the wines. But there is a catch-22; chilling a red too much reduces the sweetness and drinking a red too warm causes it to lose some of its robust flavor.

We were so comfortable with Marissa, that we gave her free reign for selecting wines for the rest of the cruise. Because she knew our interests, she recommended a wine tasting course that was offered on the ship. The course explained the difference between Old World and New World wine and ended with a blind tasting.

Old World wine is from countries or regions where winemaking first began. France, Italy, Spain, Portugal, and Germany are the premier Old World countries. New World countries are essentially the rest of the world outside of Europe. Old World country winemakers have to adhere to strict rules when making wine. France has the strictest rules of all. Only specific grapes can be grown in designated regions (referred to as appellations). They cannot irrigate even in drought. The grapes must be picked by hand and not with machinery. Add this to this to the extremely high quality, expensive oak barrels for aging and you can easily see why French wines command the price they do.

There are also strict French wine labeling laws. These can be quite complex and overwhelming for the novice and differ in the various wine regions of France. I will comment only on the Burgundy label. All red burgundy is Pinot Noire and all white burgundy is Chardonnay.

Burgundy wines are classified under rigid categories. Grand Cru is the highest quality, followed by Premier Cru, and then Communal or Village designation. This is important to know, because New World wines can put Grand Cru on their bottles at will and the consumer will think they are buying an exclusive wine. They are not. Additionally, on the Burgundy label you will find the name of the vineyard, appellation (region where only designated grapes can be grown), producer/domaine, vintage, commune/village, volume, alcohol content, and bottling data. A lot of information, but helpful if you have an interest in French wine.

A blind tasting of the Old World versus New World wines is intriguing. Some wines are easy to discern, but a clear-cut demarcation is not always recognized, as some New World winemakers are making their wines in the style of the Old World. There are some essential characteristics though. Old World wines are generally lighter, have higher acidity, less of a fruity taste, and lower alcohol content (Amarone is an exception). New World wines, for the most part, are just the opposite: heavier, lower acidity, fruity, and higher alcohol content.

There are individuals who pride themselves in drinking exclusively only Old World or New World vintages, much like those who say, "I only drink red or white." We have come to appreciate Old and New. Red and white. Wine is a living entity. Each vintage is different. You can't hold on to the bottle as it changes with age. Enjoy the moment. Pair with different foods. Live life to the fullest.

THE FRENCH CONNECTION

In the past decade, we have traveled to France on seven occasions and made it a point to visit different wine regions each time. We were fortunate to visit each of France's primary wine-producing areas: Alsace, Bordeaux, Burgundy, Loire, Provence, and the Rhône Valley.

Our first trip to France occurred after our Mediterranean cruise. That had included a trip to Monaco, but not Nice. Our traveling companions, good friends from the U.S., were Doug, a retired chemistry teacher, and Nancy, a retired nurse. Nancy, also an army brat, had spent much of her childhood in Europe and was happy to make the arrangements for what was to be a wonderful introduction to France. It was during dinner on the first night of the Rhone River cruise that we met our dear friends from Canada, Kathy and Pepe. There were two empty seats at our dinner table and they asked to join us. Our interests coincided; we were all professionals in medicine and science, enjoyed traveling, and loved wine. That was the beginning of a warm and wonderful friendship that has endured for many years. All of our subsequent trips to Europe have been with Kathy and Pepe.

The first wine region of France that we toured was Provence. Historically, this area of Southeastern France was the first Roman province just over the Alps from Italy, hence the name, Provincia Romana, from which the present name is derived. No doubt this was one of the first Roman producing vineyards dating well over two millennia.

Provence is noteworthy for another reason besides wine. Vincent Van Gogh, the famous painter, came to southern France in the late nineteenth century in search of sunlight and inspiration. The Dutch painter was intrigued with the area because of its vivid colors and Cyprus trees. Sites are marked in the vicinity of his famous paintings. The *Starry Night*, for example, was painted while looking at the Rhône in Provence.

The wine regions of Provence produce both red and white varieties, but 75% is rosé, their magnum opus. There are over 500 wineries on only 68,000 acres (27,500 hectares). It would take you almost a year-and-a-half in Provence alone if you sampled a winery a day.

An amazing surprise, in the Provencal countryside was Châteauneuf-du-Pape. The ruined, papal summer palace dominates the small village. The name means pope's new castle. This was the seat of the Roman Catholic Church when it resided in Avignon from 1309-1377. The wine bares this imposing name. Châteauneuf-du-Pape is a wine that every newcomer to French wine needs to taste. The primary grape is Grenache, but it is blended with one or two other varietals (Grenache is one of 13 different grapes grown in this appellation). Therefore, you get an amazing variety of choices from the blending of these grapes.

This wine also has a high alcohol content for an Old World wine. The average vintage in years past was about 12.5% alcohol, but with global warming, it is currently between 14.5 and 16%. For this reason, this wine needs to be decanted at least one hour before serving. Also, do not serve this wine at room temperature. 60 to 65 degrees Fahrenheit is best. The taste of this wine is spicy, rich, and bold. Some of the varieties that I tasted had definite hints of berries. I am particularly fond of raspberries and strawberries and being a novice to this new introduction, even I could appreciate these flavors.

On the northern Rhône in the Southeast of France, is a region of steep, terraced vineyards. It is in this steep and narrow valley that strong winds blow through accounting for the fluctuating temperate which impact the wine flavors. These steep, craggy hillsides characterized by limestone, rocky clay soil, and an abundance of minerals also contribute to the incredible wine produced here. The only red grape grown on these slopes is Syrah. It was in this region that we first drank the vintages of Hermitage and Côte-Rôtie.

Provence and the Rhône River excursion was our introduction to these fabulous French wines. We quickly realized that we had only visited one small region of France and it sparked our interest in learning more about French wine. We knew that winemaking in France was complex, but we had no idea that there were so many different regions, so many different grapes, and so many different combinations. We began this adventure with a very basic knowledge of winemaking. We ended this adventure with a desire to learn more.

One of our favorite areas in France is the Loire Valley and it's only a two-hour drive from Paris. This region resides along the central stretch of the Loire River, the longest river in France traversing 634 miles. There are vineyards on both sides of the river as well as countless castles and châteaux, each with a unique history to tell. For those interested in learning the French language, this is the region that speaks the purest French.

The Loire Valley has over 4,000 wineries, divided into three major growing areas that produce a wide variety of high-quality wine. More than half of all Loire wines are white. This is such a huge region to explore and an area that we have only scratched the surface. Perhaps the most well-known wine of the area is Sancerre. We were introduced to this wine for the first time while in Paris with our good friend Doug. We are sad in his departure and each time we drink this wine, we have wonderful memories of Doug and our friendship. Sancerre became popular when introduced in Parisian bistros in the 1970s. It is now synonymous with Sauvignon Blanc, which is the green skinned grape variety it is made from. This is my all-time favorite wine to have with seafood.

Again, this area is so large and has so many different wines. Only having been there twice (anxious to return again and again), we will only share our first, fabulous introductions. We loved the middle Loire. The vineyards neighboring Angers and Tours produce Chenin Blanc, the principal white grape of the region. The most incredible sparking wines come from this region. Unfortunately, most never leave here. We bring back to the States as much as we can carry (will explain in greater detail later how this is done).

Although Champagne is the most famous sparkling wine to come out of France, there are laws that protect the name Champagne. Champagne is used exclusively for sparking wines that come from the province that bears this name in Northeastern France. The Loire Valley produces many excellent sparkling wines that cannot be called Champagne. When you visit this region, do not overlook them.

Wonderful reds are also produced in the Loire Valley, such as Cabernet Franc, Cabernet Sauvignon, Pineau d'Aunis, Malbec, Gamay, Grolleau, and Pinot Noir. Again, everyone's experience will be different but I can guarantee you won't be disappointed.

Speaking of red wines, Bordeaux (the city, the region, and the wine all share the same name) was our next touring region. Over 85% of the wine produced in this area is red. There are more than 10,000 winegrowers in Bordeaux (the region – there are none in the city) alone. Magnificent estates of Lafite Rothschild, Angelus, and Haut-Brion reside in the region.

The story of Bordeaux wine is further complicated by geography. The Gironde Estuary (the largest in Europe) is formed when the Dordogne and the Garonne Rivers meet. The estuary is just downstream from the port city of Bordeaux. The landmasses on either side of the estuary are called the Left Bank and the Right Bank. All Bordeaux wine is produced here.

The Left and Right Banks are important to understand if you are drinking Bordeaux wine. Red Bordeaux is made from blending Cabernet Sauvignon and Merlot wines together. If the winery resides on the Left Bank, the blend made will have more Cabernet Sauvignon than Merlot. If the winery is located on the Right Bank, there will be more Merlot in the blend than Cabernet Sauvignon.

The Left Bank is the grand old masters. This is where the splendid Châteaux are found and where the Cabernet dominant wines bring exorbitant prices, such as Mouton Rothschild, Haut-Brion, and Lafite. These wines are best aged and increase in value and taste with time. The Right Bank had been second tier for Bordeaux wine until Robert Parker, an American writer, predicted the superiority of the Bordeaux vintage in 1982. This was his claim to fame. Parker, a lawyer, fiction writer, and now the most influential wine critic in the United States, brought accolades and praise to the Merlot producers on the Right Bank.

There are five major wine regions in Bordeaux. Pomerol is the smallest but deserves special mention. The wine produced here is a blend with Merlot and Cabernet Franc. The wines made in this region are some of the most amazing blends. The most prestigious Pomerol estate is Château Pétrus. It's a 17-acre (seven hectares) vineyard. It differs from the others in this region, since their wines are all Merlot. This wine is referred to in the motion picture *Red*. The humorous line in the movie is, "How do you torture a Frenchmen?" Followed by the answer, "Break his bottle of Petrus!" This is what they did – in fact, they broke quite a few bottles. Petrus is sold for around $3,000 to $4,000 a bottle depending on the vintage year.

Saint-Émilion is a quintessential wine town to visit before leaving Bordeaux. Some of the most esteemed, expensive wines are purchased here. The town is quaint with its narrow, cobblestone streets, Romanesque church, and 13th century tower. The wine shops are elegant. Kathy and Pepe were very anxious to visit the town and buy wine to ship back home. We never experienced such an extraordinary tasting. Needless to say, we all bought wine to send back to our respective homes.

Burgundy (Bourgogne in French) is a historic and highly esteemed wine region in Eastern France. It is legendary for its legacy of red Burgundy (100% Pinot Noir) and white Burgundy (100% Chardonnay). Chablis is a variant of Chardonnay. Instead of being aged in oak barrels, the grapes are fermented in stainless steel vats, producing a lighter-bodied white wine. Do the Pinot Noir wines from California taste like French Burgundy? Ideally, it is the same grape. However, the answer is no. The West coast wines are sweet and fruity, which is very different from any real French Burgundy. If you don't believe me, you are welcome to try for yourself. It will cost you though. Excellent French Burgundy is some of the most expensive wine in the world.

Alsace has an incredible, tumultuous history. Separated from Germany by the Rhine River, this region has been an area of constant dispute between these two countries for centuries. The region was originally under French rule with Charlemagne in the 9th century. It became part of Germany during the time of the Holy Roman Empire. The Thirty Years' War ended with a peace agreement in 1648, giving the region back to France. Following the Franco-Prussian War in 1871, Alsace-Lorraine (Elsass-Lothringen in German) was the name given to this territory that was again relinquished by France to Germany. The region was returned to France after World War I, then acquired by Germany in 1940 at the beginning of World War II, and finally surrendered back to France at the end of the war in 1945.

We have traveled through this region on several occasions with various guides. We have noticed that the German guides are passionately German with disdain for the French and the French guides are passionately French with little regard for the Germans. It is reminiscent of the feud between the Hatfield's and the McCoy's.

The vast majority of wines produced in Alsace are white. This is the one region of France where the wine is not named after the place of origin, but rather the principal grape variety from which the wine is produced. Pinot Blanc, Pinot Gris, and Riesling are very popular and excellent wines in this region. But my all-time favorite in Alsace is the Gewürztraminer. I believe it is one of the best that I have ever tasted. I guess I am exhibiting a little snobbery, but the preeminent New World Gewürztraminer does not compare to the varietal produced in Alsace. Gewürztraminer is a pink grape that originated in Germany. It grows best in cooler climates. Over several hundreds of years, the vineyards planted with this grape have now expanded and completely circumscribe the Alps. Out of all of these regions, Alsace is the world's largest producer of Gewürztraminer. For the best quality of this wine in Alsace, look for the designation, Grand Cru on the label and Haut-Rhin, the area with the highest number of Grand Cru vineyards.

Our introduction and appreciation of French wine has gradually developed over the past decade with our numerous trips to France. Our experience has been most rewarding when we have gone to wineries and tastings that we booked ahead, gone in smaller groups, showed an interest in their particular product, and demonstrated proper wine etiquette. A busload of people going to a vineyard for a wine tasting is on par with taking a group of elementary school children to a museum. At the end of the day, you will have seen a lot of stuff, but you will not have learned very much.

Our understanding has been that you can walk into tiny little wine shops and grocery stores in France and get wonderful wines that are very inexpensive, especially when paired with the local food. On many occasions, we have enjoyed a fabulous light lunch with French wine, cheese, olives, and bread that we purchased in the spur of the moment at a small local shop or market. That is not always the case when you buy French wine in the U.S. We have dined in very fine restaurants and ordered higher priced French wine and been very disappointed. Price does not necessarily reflect quality. A $100 bottle of French wine in the U.S. is not equal to a $100 bottle in France. There is considerable markup in restaurants, plus the cost of exportation. How carefully the wines are managed in shipping and even the proper storage in the U.S. are also factors in enjoying these wines at their best. Our finest food parings with French wine have definitely been in France, because the best French wines never leave France. We truly believe the French export the best of their worst.

THINGS WE HAVE LEARNED

Since good French wine never leaves France, the question arises, how can we legally smuggle it out? I'm being facetious, but the answer is yes, you can bring back really good French wine to the U.S. Leslie solved the problem. She had me weigh our suitcases with our packed clothing for the trip. You are permitted to carry 50 pounds in each suitcase when traveling by air without additional charges. She instructed me that we could take no more than 25 pounds in each traveling bag. Why? Six bottles of wine weigh approximately 24 pounds. We need to keep the suitcase weight limit just less than 50 pounds when returning to the States.

The next question is how do you package six bottles of wine safely in a suitcase? The answer is wine diapers. These are reusable, protective, absorbent sleeves that you slip the wine bottle into. Diapering your wine bottles protects against breakage and if the bottle should break, the padded diaper sleeve will absorb the liquid. You can carry one case of excellent French wine in two suitcases. Two cases of wine in four suitcases. That's what we've done for the past 10 years. In all of our travels, we have never had a broken bottle. We always declare the wine on the U.S. Customs form and so far, we have never had to pay a Customs fee when returning to the U.S. Most importantly, our guests are amazed at the French wines we bring back. They repeatedly remark that they have never tasted French wines like these in the States. It is true; the best are smuggled out of France!

After our wonderful excursions in France, we are overwhelmed at the hundreds of combinations of both red and white wine that are being produced. Each vineyard is unique and each vintage has something different to offer. No two red wines or white wines are alike. All varieties of wine have something to offer. Now can you see why a statement of "I only drink red or I only drink white" is limiting? These remarks frequently come from individuals who have little understanding of wine appreciation.

If I learned anything from the French, it's that wine is not meant to be drunk without food. And I agree. The wine's flavor is remarkably enhanced with food and food is extraordinarily enhanced with wine. The French serve wine primarily with meals and don't typically drink it socially.

It is also important to know the difference between Champagne and sparkling wines. They are made the same way, but they are not called by the same name. Only a sparkling wine from the region of Champagne can be called Champagne. If you are drinking a sparkling wine not from this region, do not say, "I really like this Champagne!" Rather say, "I like this sparkling wine." The same is true with the Italian sparkling, Prosecco. Call it what it is – Prosecco.

It is intriguing how knowledge often comes about in unusual ways. During President Barack Obama's State of the Union address in 2015, Supreme Court Justice Ruth Bader Ginsburg appeared to fall asleep. This was captured on national television. They interviewed the 81-year-old Justice and she admitted that she may have had too much of a very good wine. They asked her what wine she was drinking and my ears perked up. She replied, "Opus One, 2012." For our anniversary that year, I purchased a bottle of Opus One Cabernet Sauvignon, 2012 for $256. At present, this same vintage is selling for $850 a bottle. Leslie prepared a wonderful anniversary meal and we opened the wine and sipped and savored it all night. It was fabulous. Interestingly, I received a shipment of a Cabernet Sauvignon, 2012 from a vineyard in Sonoma Valley, in California the next day. I paid $48 a bottle for this Cab that I had never tasted before. I read the blend on the label and it was almost the same as the Opus One we had the night before. I asked Leslie to prepare a similar meal so we could compare the two wines. The second bottle was not better, but it was certainly comparable to the Opus One. We enjoyed it as much as the Opus One from the night before. You can't always judge a wine by its price tag.

A wine made from the same grape is called varietal. A wine maker may mix grapes from different plots or even export the same grape from other areas, but the mixture will still be a single grape. To be classified as a varietal in the U.S., the wine must contain at least 75% of one grape type. The percentage in Europe for a varietal is 80%.

The vast majority of red wines are not varietals, but blends. On average, blends contain 40-50% of one grape type and a smaller mixture of usually one or two additional grape varieties. The grape varieties and the percent of the mixture are printed on the label of the bottle. There is considerable information that can be gleaned simply from reading the label.

Why are wines blended? Blending can enhance the flavor, aroma, and even the texture of the wine. The final product is a complex wine that is improved and better appreciated. Winemakers blend to enrich and develop the qualities they desire. The result they are trying to achieve is a superior wine. It is quite an art and the reason certain wineries are held in higher esteem than others.

Speaking of blending, one night we were having an impromptu dinner gathering after having been out of the country for some time. We knew we were short on wine. We had three different mediocre bottles of red wine that I was too embarrassed to serve. In retrospect, I don't know why I did what I did. I made a cuvée, a blend of wines. Before they arrived, I decanted all three bottles together. The irony of ironies, I had nothing but compliments on the wine. Thank goodness no one asked for the name. I simply smiled when they told me that I really knew wine! I cannot promise that you will get the same results if you do the same, but you may like to try.

An enjoyable experience to have with friends is to purchase three bottles of a particular wine a year apart in age. Start by opening the youngest bottle and have your guests taste the wine. Proceed with the second oldest year and compare. Finally, try the oldest bottle. I guarantee even neophytes to wine will appreciate and notice the difference in taste.

Another great undertaking with your friends is to purchase the same wine from three different wineries. You can choose different price ranges or compare three different wines of roughly the same price. Palates will vary. Not everyone will agree and often these tastings will stimulate enjoyable discussions.

On the practical side, can a half bottle of wine be saved for another day? We enjoy a glass of wine each night with our evening meal. There are 25 ounces in each bottle. We have found that if I pour each of us a 4-ounce glass of wine from the wine refrigerator, re-cork it immediately, and put it into the standard refrigerator (colder – mid 30 degrees F.), the wine keeps well for an additional two days. Yes, we can get three servings for the two of us from one bottle! The immediate re-corking and refrigeration markedly slows down oxidation which delays wine spoilage. There are inexpensive devices that are easy to use to pump out a little of the air that enters when you pour out your glasses and then re-cork. Allegedly, they say you can get an extra couple of days before the wine goes bad. If you use these devices (there are several available), you still need to refrigerate the wine immediately.

The ultimate wine preserver is a Coravin device that punctures a hollow needle through the cork and then releases a cartridge of argon gas (inert) into the bottle to replace the air (displaces the oxygen). These devices, along with the argon replacement cartridges, are rather expensive. If you aren't drinking a relatively expensive bottle of wine, you are spending more on the argon than the wine you are trying to save.

Our journey with wine has taken us all over the world. We have enjoyed wine throughout Europe and both North and South

America. We can honestly say that there have been few disappointments. Sure, there are regions that are our favorites, but each new wine we drink opens us up to another culture and new friendships. As the Psalmist David said, "*and wine to gladden the heart of man*" (Psalm 104.1).

RED WINE – A BASIC FOOD GROUP

When we think of wine, the first thing that comes to mind is an alcoholic beverage. Put that thought aside and consider this – grapes have a natural tendency to ferment in nature without mankind's intervention. Martin Luther said it best as, "Beer is made by men, wine by God." The resulting product – red wine, contains many beneficial nutrients among which are antioxidants (flavonoids, polyphenols, and resveratrol). While there are some vitamins and minerals present, it is true, they are not high. Alcohol is the culprit in wine that has the negative connotation with regard to health benefits. There are two sides to every coin and, as a physician, I would like to present the positive benefits of all of the above, including EtOH (alcohol).

Many scientists believe that moderate consumption of red wine is protective against heart disease and some forms of cancer. One chemical component thought to be responsible for this are catechins, also known as flavonoids[2]. They are directly linked to the tannins in red wine. Tannins reside in the skin of the grapes. Red wines are fermented with the grape skins, which gives the wine its characteristic red color. In addition, they provide the beneficial plant compounds so important to heart health. Grapes for producing white wine have their skins removed, so many of the important nutrients are present in much smaller amounts or not present at all.

How do flavonoids work? Oxidation is a chemical reaction that occurs in our bodies producing *free radicals,* or unstable molecules. These free radicals attack our organ systems and do unremitting damage. This oxidation reaction (also known as oxidative stress) causes us to age, alters healthy cells into cancerous ones, contributes to elevated blood pressure, hardening of the arteries, and promotion of inflammatory conditions like arthritis, to name a few. Flavonoids are believed to function as antioxidants, thus preventing free radical molecules from doing cellular damage.

Red wine also contains resveratrol, another highly important natural antioxidant that has received a lot of attention. Evidence suggests that this antioxidant may boost the immune system, decrease inflammation, block cancer formation, protect against heart disease, and promote longevity. Interest in this antioxidant has intensified as it has been implemented in cognitive health as well. Memory, focus, attention, and learning are being studied. The evidence is not certain, but avenues of research are looking into the neuroprotective effects in that resveratrol may protect against Alzheimer's and dementia. In all fairness, most of the studies have been in the laboratory with animal models.

Resveratrol in red wine may also have anti-clotting factors that help decrease our risk for blood clots and strokes. Resveratrol is sold as a dietary supplement. It can contain anywhere from 1 milligram (mg) to 500 mg per capsule or tablet. It is important to note that this anti-oxidant could interact with prescription anti-coagulants (blood thinners), thereby increasing your risk for bleeding. I would caution, more is not better. It is not known whether there is a safe or effective dosage. I would not recommend taking these supplements, but a glass of red wine is not in this category.

In the past, drinking wine has been associated with a higher risk of hypertension (high blood pressure). It is now believed that one glass of red wine a day seems to protect those with hypertension. It helps to regulate cholesterol levels in the blood by reducing the low-density lipoproteins (bad cholesterol) and increasing the high-density lipoproteins (good cholesterol). Even the American Heart Association has stated that moderate alcohol consumption may prevent the formation of plaque or blockage in the arteries.

From watching TV medical shows, most people are aware that conversations take place in the operating room (OR). Daily OR assignments often put a team together that works with a surgeon in a particular room for several operations. A routine crew consists of an anesthesia person, often more that one nurse, and surgical assistants, the number depending on the complexity of the case. Some operations are long, but fairly routine. As we work together, if all is going well, we engage in various conversations.

I recall one such conversation several years ago. The subject of wine came up and my surgical assistant asked me if the alcohol in red wine was a major factor for keeping the arteries free from plaque and thereby reducing one's risk of heart attack and stroke? Before I could answer, my anesthesiologist, very much a tea-to-taller, was quick to answer, "You can get the same results from grape juice." I countered, "I agree, grape juice contains flavonoids and anti-oxidants which are heart healthy, but that was not the question. I refer you back to Chemistry 101. EtOH is an important solvent in both inorganic and organic chemistry. It readily dissolves essential oils, esters, fatty acids, hydrocarbons, resins, and soaps. Therefore, the answer to the question is, it certainly contributes." He didn't answer.

The French Paradox is a familiar concept that has been widely discussed. It was coined in the 1980s by French scientists to describe the phenomenon of low coronary heart disease in France despite a diet rich in saturated fat. Red wine was touted as the major contributor that bolstered this phenomenon. Since then, hundreds of scientists have weighed in on this hypothesis with many different and varying opinions. A major flaw that has been uncovered by the World Health Organization is that French physicians under-reported heart disease deaths. Even in light of this disclosure, there are still positive issues that we can draw from this paradox.

Many Americans have heard of the French Paradox and the

mental picture they draw is a country that drinks a lot of red wine, consumes untold quantities of croissants, baguettes, butter, cream, and cheese and yet is thin and healthy. This is not a valid perception.

The majority of the French drink moderate amounts of red wine mostly with meals. They adhere to, essentially, a healthy Mediterranean diet. Not only do they eat small portions, they eat and drink slowly and enjoy the complimented wine with their food. In addition, they have far more self-discipline than Americans. They rarely snack between meals and their daily activities are abound with walking and bike riding.

There are myriads of studies showing that moderate consumption of red wine can be beneficial to your health. It also needs to be pointed out that heavy drinking can result in permanent, irreversible damage to organ systems, particularly the liver and the brain. Moderation is the key to almost everything in life. It is not abstinence but rather the avoidance of extremes. Only one book in the Hebrew Bible (Old Testament) fails to mention wine or vineyards and that is the Book of Jonah. The earliest historical record of viniculture in the Hebrew Bible is the account of Noah and his unforeseen inebriation. Some religious sects use this story to advocate abstaining from alcohol all together. Rather than a story about abstinence, I understand the narrative to be a warning about overindulgence. It is noteworthy that the Bible has far more to say about gluttony than intoxication.

FINAL WORDS

When we began our journey with wine, more than a decade ago, we knew very little about fine wine. Developing a more refined palate and appreciating all kinds of wine did not happen overnight. Everyone is born with more than 10,000 taste buds, and yet so many people have restricted gastronomic preferences.

The majority of Americans responding to various poles have repetitively listed the following wines as their most popular wine choices: White Zinfandel, Moscato, Chardonnay (sweet New World), Pinot Grigio (it is really Pinot Gris unless it came from Italy), and Merlot The vast majority purchases their wine in grocery stores in the $10 to $15 price range. Believe it or not, the public at large chooses the wine they purchase by the fancy or colorful label and how appealingly the bottle is to them.

There are more than 10,000 different grape varieties, over 40,000 wineries, and a quarter of a million types of wine in the world. Wine is the world's oldest naturally fermented beverage. Now I ask, "Why would you chose White Zinfandel, a total fluke[3] as your favorite?" If I am labeled a *wine snob*, then I will wear the badge with pride.

Fine wine with elegant surroundings brings about a warm sensation of tranquility. Wine brings immeasurable pleasure not simply in its aroma and taste, but in its unique ability to bring people together and strengthen the bonds of love and friendship. Wine is enjoyed with simple meals as well as with fine dining. It is enjoyed at weddings, celebrations, and when meeting new friends and acquaintances.

In closing, Leslie and I have barely scratched the surface of what there is to know about wine. We continue to ask questions and try to learn more. We encourage anyone who is interested in wine to not be intimidated, make inquiries, and above all, enjoy. We hope our passion will be contagious and you will come to love and appreciate wine as we have.

GLOSSARY OF WINE TERMS

Acidity
Is one of 5 central traits in every wine - the others being tannins, alcohol, sweetness, and body. All wines are acidic ranging from 2.5-4.5 pH. Acidity in wine is the tartness you perceive in your mouth. A good example of acidity is lemonade.

Alcohol
The end product of the fermentation of natural grape sugars by yeast is ethyl alcohol; wine ranges from 5.5% to as high as 20%; higher alcohol levels tend to taste bolder, while lower levels have lighter-bodied taste.

Appellation
In France, this is a legally defined region where strict restrictions are placed on the vineyards and wineries. They are permitted to grow only certain grapes, given maximum yields, as well as other quality factors that are firmly enforced.

Blend
The process of combining two or more grape varieties after each has been individually fermented; most red wines are blends.

Body
A tasting term that refers to the perceived weight of a wine on the palate; a number of factors determine the body, such as the grape variety, tannins, alcohol content, etc. The body is referred to as full bodied, medium bodied, or light bodied.

Color
A wine's color can tell you a lot about the wine you are drinking. Color comes from the contact and the amount of time exposed to the grape skins. White wine is not in contact with grape skins but can have color if aged in oak barrels. Color can also tell you about a wine's age. Red wines turn brownish orange with age and white wines become darker.

Cru
A French term simply translated as *growth*. It is predominately used as a status term meaning that the particular vineyard, winery, or estate has met specific, high quality standards.

Dry
A dry wine is one that has no residual sugar after fermentation. All red wines are dry. Never say, "I'd like a dry red!"

Grand Cru
This is a French term that means *great growth*. Grand Cru designates the highest level in the vineyard classification. Only 2% of all Burgundy is Grand Cru.

Legs
Wine legs, or *tears of wine* as the French say, are drops of wine that run down the inside of the glass after swirling the wine. The phenomenon is caused by the evaporation of alcohol that affects the surface tension of a liquid. A wine with higher alcohol content will have longer legs.

Nose
This term is synonymous with bouquet; it is the summation of a wine's fragrances or aromas.

Premier Cru
French for *first growth*. This is a good wine, but not in the category

of Grand Cru.

Reserve
This is an American term meaning a high quality wine. There are no legally binding regulations. The term can be very misleading. Often this term is placed on cheaper bottles of wine as a marketing tool.

Sommelier
This is a highly trained, professional wine steward. They have a vast knowledge of wine and are often credentialed.

Tannins
These are phenolic compounds that are present in most plants. Tannins are predominately in the skins of the grape. They are astringents and give structure to the wine. As wine ages, the tannins diminish making the wine less harsh.

Terroir
A French term used to describe the natural environment of the soil, sunlight, topography, climate, and any other factors that influence the ultimate character of the wine.

Vintage
It pertains to a certain year a wine is produced; a particular harvest.

Viticulture
The science of growing grapes for wine.

Varietal
A wine made principally from one grape.

THUMBNAIL SKETCH OF WINES

Amarone
Considered by many to be one of Italy's best red wines. It is produced in northern Italy and made primarily from Corvina grapes that are dried on racks before pressing. The alcohol content is high (minimum 14%) and the wine is rarely released before five years of aging.

Beaujolais
This wine is made from the Gamay grape in the Beaujolais region of France, just north of Lyon. The grape skins are very thin, so the wine is low in tannins. The wine has a medium red color, light body, and fruity flavors.

This is not to be confused with Beaujolais Nouveau; a wine that is quickly fermented and drunk immediately after the harvest. Barrels are rolled through the streets and this wine is drunk for celebration.

Bordeaux
A city on the Garonne River in Southwest France, as well as a large wine-producing region. It produces one of the most famous and coveted wine blends in the world. The red wine is made mostly from Cabernet Sauvignon, Merlot, and Cabernet Franc, while a white wine is made from Sauvignon Blanc and Semillon.

Burgundy

A renowned wine producing region in Eastern France. It produces what is probably the most romanticized red wine in the world. Pinot Noir is the sole grape used for making red Burgundy and Chardonnay is the single grape used for producing white Burgundy.

Cabernet Franc
A red grape common to Bordeaux in France and mainly used in blends. Winemakers add it to Merlot and Cabernet Sauvignon-based wines to make the red wine more complex and full-bodied. It is not common, but it can be used as a single-varietal wine.

Cabernet Sauvignon
This is probably the most well known red grape in the world. It originated in Bordeaux, France but grows well in warmer climates. It produces a dry, red wine rich in color and tannins. It is extremely popular in New World vineyards. The West coast of the U.S. has popularized and built its reputation on this grape.

Chardonnay
No doubt the best-known and most extensively planted white grape in the world. This is another grape that originated in Bordeaux, France. The most popular in the U.S. is the buttery style. This is brought about by allowing the grapes to undergo malolactic fermentation in oak barrels. The other style is referred to as naked, or unoaked, which allows the true splendor of the grape to come through. To complicate things, there are blends of the two.

Chenin Blanc
A white wine grape variety native to the Loire Valley in France. It is extremely versatile and can be made into a variety of wines including still, sparkling, dry, or sweet. The West coast of the U.S. has recently been using it more in blends to add complexity, but you can find single varietal ones.

Claret
Claret is an English name for red Bordeaux. The term was first used in the Middle Age and continues in Great Britain today.

Gamay
A light and dry red table wine. The grape is used primarily in France to make Beaujolais. It is sometimes termed a picnic red but also pairs well with some Asian foods and duck. Another recommendation is with Thanksgiving turkey.

Gewürztraminer
An enjoyable, light, white wine that has an exuberant fruity taste with hints of clove spice. It originated in Germany and the grape grows best in cooler climates. The largest producers are in Alsace Lorraine in the Rhine Valley.

Grenache
This is a deep, ruby red wine that the French have championed in the southern Rhône Valley, but its origin is Spain. It is spicy but soft on the palate. The grape ripens late and likes a warm climate to grow.

Ice Wine
A wine made from frozen grapes that came originally from Germany and Austria (eiswein). Canada is also a leading producer today.

Madeira
This is a fortified wine that has been made on a Portuguese island off the coast of Morocco since the fifteenth century. This was a favorite of George Washington and Thomas Jefferson. Both men had large quantities shipped to their estates.

Malbec
A dark purple grape of French origin has an inky color with robust tannins. This is one of six grapes that the French are allowed to blend with Bordeaux wine. It is now exceedingly popular in Argentina.

Merlot
This dark, blue-colored grape originated in the Bordeaux region

of France. Its name in French means *blackbird*. It is both a blending grape and a varietal. It is now popular throughout the world, particularly in South America.

Pinot Blanc
A white wine grape is very popular in Alsace and Germany. It is a genetic mutation of the very fragile and red Pinot Noir grape. One cluster on the vine will be white while the rest of the fruit is dark. In genetics this is called a point mutation and is the origin of Pinot Blanc.

Pinot Gris
This is a white grape with a grayish colored skin (*gris* in French means gray). It is often called Pinot Grigio. They are, in fact, the same grape but differ in where they are grown. As a result, the wines produced are not exactly the same. Pinot Grigio is produced in Italy.

Pinot Noir
This is Burgundy's most famous noble grape. It is used to make both red Burgundy wines as well as clear Champagne and other sparkling wines. So, why is Champagne and sparkling wine not red? They are colorless because the skins of the Pinot Noir grape are carefully removed so the pigments in the grape skin do not stain the juice.

Pomerol
Pomerol is a red wine appellation on the right bank in the Bordeaux region. It is in this Eastern section (only 2,000 acres), on the higher elevation where Pomerol meets Saint-Émilion, that the best wines are produced. The wines produced here are a blend of Merlot (the dominate grape) and Cabernet Franc. This is the region where the most sought after Petrus is made.

Riesling
Another very popular German white wine originally from the Rhine region. It is rarely oaked and the wines are varietally pure. Riesling grapes are very aromatic with fruit or flower aromas. They can be dry or sweet.

Rosé

This is a French name meaning *pink*. Winemakers crush the grapes and then allow the juice to soak with the grape skins for a couple of days. The color then is pink and not red so it cannot be classified as a red wine. The best Rosés are made in Provence, France. Most of the Rosé wines in the U.S. tend to be cheap and of poor quality. Next time, ask for a bottle from Provence, France!

Sancerre
The Sancerre wine region is located in the Eastern part of the Loire Valley in France. This region is largely planted with Sauvignon Blanc. This is one of the best regions of the world for this wine. In addition to the perfect climate, underneath the beautiful rolling hills are rich limestone beds that contribute to the amazing flavor of this wine.

Sauternes
This wine is produced in a Bordeaux wine region that lies on the Garonne River in France. The mornings are very foggy, cool, and damp, thus a perfect environment for the Botrytis mold to develop on the grape. The mold causes the grapes to shrivel and become sugar laden. This particular grape matures late and the winegrowers intentionally leave these grapes longer on the vine to make this wonderful, sweet desert wine. Sauternes wines' honey flavor is one of its main characteristics.

Sauvignon Blanc
A white grape comes with origins in France. Both Bordeaux and the Loire Valley are two of the highest producers in the country. The grape is also extremely popular for winemakers in New Zealand. Chardonnay is a full-bodied white wine. Sauvignon Blanc, by comparison is lighter, with an herbal scent and citrus flavors.

Syrah
The birthplace of Syrah is Southeastern France; however, it is now grown all over the world. The Australians refer to this grape as *Shiraz*. It is a full-bodied wine that is heavy on the palate due to its abundant mouth-drying tannins. Wine makers cold soak the grapes for up to several weeks to reduce the tannins and make the wine less harsh. It can be found as a varietal or a blend.

Zinfandel

White Zinfandel is an anomaly. The Zinfandel black-skin grape produces a wonderfully hearty red wine. However, in the U.S., White Zinfandel is preferred six to one. It was produced by accident in California in the 1970s by winemaker Bob Trinchero at Sutter Home Winery. The winery was trying to make a deeper red Zinfandel and skimmed off over 500 gallons of the juice that that had been soaking with the grape skins for a few days after the grapes were pressed. The intention was to make a richer wine by allowing greater exposure of the skins to less liquid. As a frugal after thought, the winery decided to sell off the early-decanted light wine. Most people do not know that the product they made was actually a Rosé. It had a light bluish-pink color with a dry taste. They called it White Zinfandel because they did not think people would consider this a quality Rosé. The Sutter Home Winery sold the new wine with some success. Later, another unforeseen accident occurred. The yeast died before converting all of the sugar to alcohol. The residual sugar in this fermentation resulted in a very sweet wine. In the U.S., this became an overnight success. They now could make a very cheep wine, which the American public loved.

[1] One reason for the high cost of French oak is its scarcity. During the Napoleonic Wars many French forests were cut down to build warships.

[2] Flavonoids are isolated from plants. There are over 8,000 known compounds. They exhibit biological activity as anti-oxidants, antimicrobials, antiviral, anti-inflammatory, antiallergenic, and vasodilating agents.

[3] See explanation of why White Zinfandel is a poor choice in the *Thumbnail Sketch of Wines*

AFTERWORD

The information in this book has come about after a decade of learning and enjoying wine. The idea for the book has been many months in the making. The actual manuscript was written while Leslie and I were quarantined during the pandemic of 2020. It was thirty days well spent. I hope you agree.

Please consider leaving a review.

ACKNOWLEDGEMENT

This book would not have happened without the encouragement and knowledge of three very good friends who are no longer with us. It is dedicated to the memories of Mary Curtis, Steve Preston and Doug Birchmeier. We miss you all.

Thanks to Maggie Fulmer and Sara McIntosh for your brilliant editing. You took my ideas to the next level!

Thanks to my beautiful Soulmate! You stayed the course. I love you.

ABOUT THE AUTHOR

L Michael Lavender

 Michael Lavender is a retired MD/PhD living in Kentucky and Maine. His wife Leslie is a retired Family Nurse Practitioner. They are happily enjoying their retirement learning about all the things they didn't have time for durig their busy working lives.

Printed in Dunstable, United Kingdom